Teaching Little Fingers to Play More Hymns

Piano Solos with Optional Teacher Accompaniments

Arranged by Glenda Austin

T0081634

CONTENTS

ISBN 978-1-5400-2783-2

WILLIS MUSIC

EXCLUSIVELY DISTRIBUTED BY

7777 W. BLUEMOUND RD. P.O. BOX 13819 MILWAUKEE, WI 53213

Visit Hal Leonard Online at
www.halleonard.com

How Firm a Foundation
Optional Teacher Accompaniment

Arr. Glenda Austin

How Firm a Foundation

Rippon's selection of hymns, 1787

Early American
Arr. Glenda Austin

Play both hands one octave higher when performing as a duet.

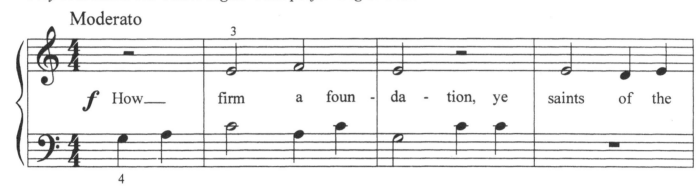

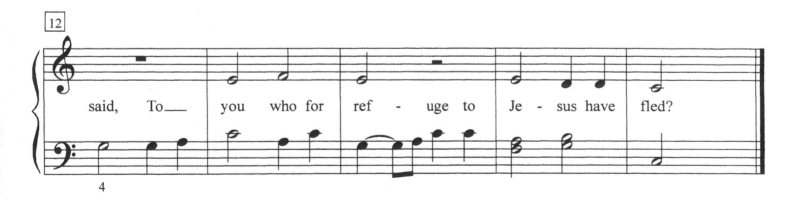

I've Been Redeemed
Optional Teacher Accompaniment

Arr. Glenda Austin

I've Been Redeemed

Traditional

Unknown
Arr. Glenda Austin

Play both hands one octave higher when performing as a duet.

Spirited

f I've been re - deemed by the blood of the Lamb.

I've been re - deemed by the blood of the Lamb.

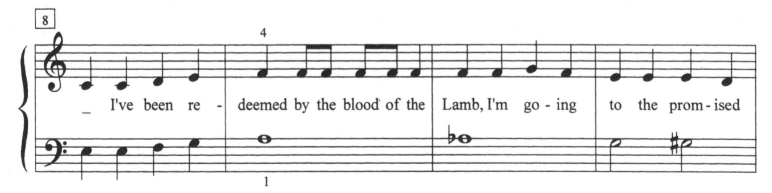

I've been re - deemed by the blood of the Lamb, I'm go - ing to the prom - ised

land. All my sins are washed a - way, I've been re - deemed!

Come, Thou Almighty King

Optional Teacher Accompaniment

Arr. Glenda Austin

Come, Thou Almighty King

Unknown

Felice de Giardini
Arr. Glenda Austin

Play both hands one octave higher when performing as a duet.

Brethren, We Have Met to Worship

Optional Teacher Accompaniment

Arr. Glenda Austin

Brethren, We Have Met to Worship

George Atkins

William Moore
Arr. Glenda Austin

Play both hands one octave higher when performing as a duet.

Breth - ren, we have met to wor - ship and a - dore the Lord our God;

Will you pray with all your pow - er, while we try to preach the Word?

All is vain un - less the Spi - rit of the Ho - ly One comes down;

Breth - ren pray, and ho - ly man - na will be show - ered

all a - round.

Just As I Am
Optional Teacher Accompaniment

Arr. Glenda Austin

Just As I Am

Charlotte Elliott

William B. Bradbury
Arr. Glenda Austin

Play both hands one octave higher when performing as a duet.

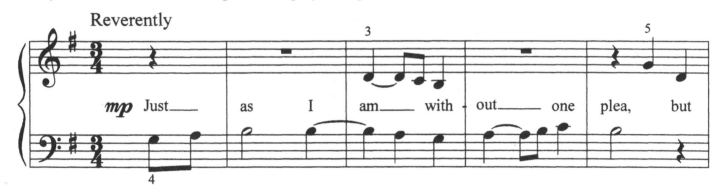

All Hail the Power of Jesus' Name

Optional Teacher Accompaniment

Arr. Glenda Austin

All Hail the Power of Jesus' Name

Edward Perronet

James Ellor
Arr. Glenda Austin

Play both hands one octave higher when performing as a duet.

Majestically

Great Is Thy Faithfulness
Optional Teacher Accompaniment

Arr. Glenda Austin

Great Is Thy Faithfulness

William Runyan

Thomas Chisholm
Arr. Glenda Austin

Play both hands one octave higher when performing as a duet.

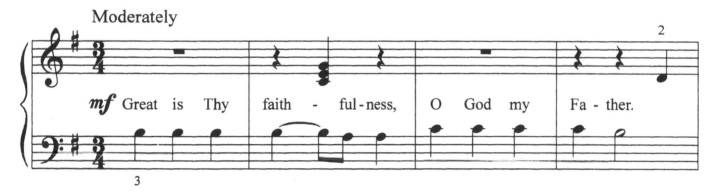

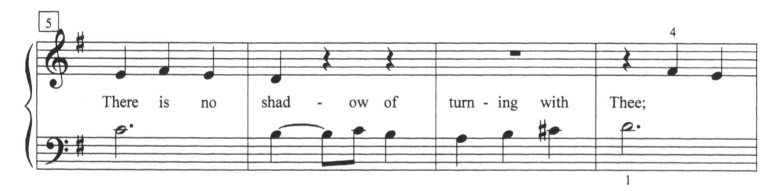

Accompaniment

O God, Our Help in Ages Past
Optional Teacher Accompaniment

Arr. Glenda Austin

O God, Our Help in Ages Past

Isaac Watts

William Croft
Arr. Glenda Austin

Play both hands one octave higher when performing as a duet.

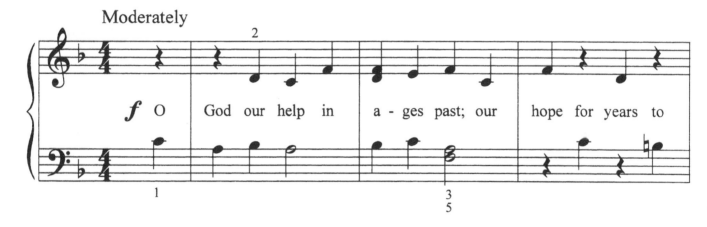

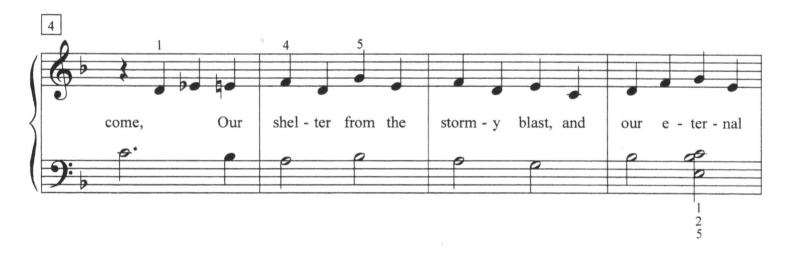

Come, Christians, Join to Sing

Optional Teacher Accompaniment

Arr. Glenda Austin

Come, Christians, Join to Sing

Christian Henry Bateman

Traditional Melody
Arr. Glenda Austin

Play both hands one octave higher when performing as a duet.

Stately

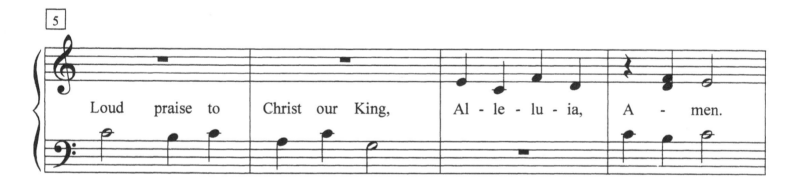

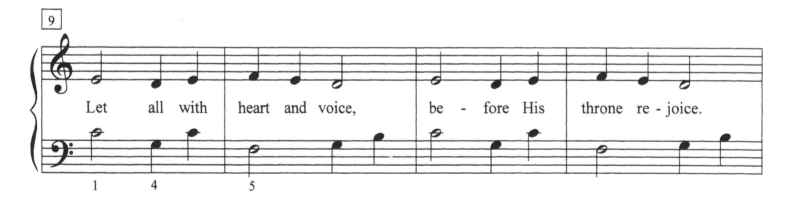

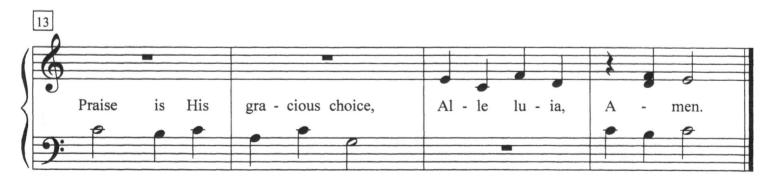

'Tis So Sweet to Trust in Jesus
Optional Teacher Accompaniment

Arr. Glenda Austin

Serenely

'Tis So Sweet to Trust in Jesus

Louisa M. R. Stead

William J. Kirkpatrick
Arr. Glenda Austin

Play both hands one octave higher when performing as a duet.

Serenely

mf 'Tis so sweet___ to trust in Je-sus, Just to take___ Him at His word,

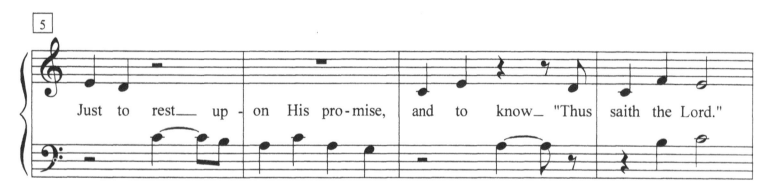

Just to rest___ up-on His pro-mise, and to know___ "Thus saith the Lord."

Je-sus, Je-sus, how I trust Him, How I've praised___ Him o'er and o'er.

Je-sus, Je-sus, pre - cious Je-sus, O for grace___ to trust Him more!

Teaching Little Fingers to Play More

TEACHING LITTLE FINGERS TO PLAY MORE
by Leigh Kaplan
Teaching Little Fingers to Play More is a fun-filled and colorfully illustrated follow-up book to *Teaching Little Fingers to Play*. It strengthens skills learned while carefully easing the transition into John Thompson's *Modern Course, First Grade*.
00406137 Book only $6.99
00406527 Book/Audio $9.99

SUPPLEMENTARY SERIES
All books include optional teacher accompaniments.

BROADWAY SONGS
arr. Carolyn Miller
MID TO LATER ELEMENTARY LEVEL
10 great show tunes for students to enjoy, including: Edelweiss • I Whistle a Happy Tune • I Won't Grow Up • Maybe • The Music of the Night • and more.
00416928 Book only $6.99
00416929 Book/Audio $12.99

CHILDREN'S SONGS
arr. Carolyn Miller
MID-ELEMENTARY LEVEL
10 songs: The Candy Man • Do-Re-Mi • I'm Popeye the Sailor Man • It's a Small World • Linus and Lucy • The Muppet Show Theme • Sesame Street Theme • Supercalifragilisticexpialidocious • Tomorrow.
00416810 Book only $6.99
00416811 Book/Audio $12.99

CLASSICS
arr. Randall Hartsell
MID-ELEMENTARY LEVEL
7 solos: Marche Slave • Over the Waves • Polovtsian Dance (from the opera *Prince Igor*) • Pomp and Circumstance • Rondeau • Waltz (from the ballet *Sleeping Beauty*) • William Tell Overture.
00406760 Book only $5.99
00416513 Book/Audio $10.99

DISNEY TUNES
arr. Glenda Austin
MID-ELEMENTARY LEVEL
9 songs, including: Circle of Life • Colors of the Wind • A Dream Is a Wish Your Heart Makes • A Spoonful of Sugar • Under the Sea • A Whole New World • and more.
00416750 Book only $9.99
00416751 Book/Audio $12.99

EASY DUETS
arr. Carolyn Miller
MID-ELEMENTARY LEVEL
9 equal-level duets: A Bicycle Built for Two • Blow the Man Down • Chopsticks • Do Your Ears Hang Low? • I've Been Working on the Railroad • The Man on the Flying Trapeze • Short'nin' Bread • Skip to My Lou • The Yellow Rose of Texas.
00416832 Book only $6.99
00416833 Book/Audio $10.99

JAZZ AND ROCK
Eric Baumgartner
MID-ELEMENTARY LEVEL
11 solos, including: Big Bass Boogie • Crescendo Rock • Funky Fingers • Jazz Waltz in G • Rockin' Rhythm • Squirrel Race • and more!
00406765 Book only $5.99

MOVIE MUSIC
arr. Carolyn Miller
LATER ELEMENTARY LEVEL
10 magical movie arrangements: Bella's Lullaby (Twilight) • Somewhere Out There (An American Tail) • True Love's Kiss (Enchanted) • and more.
00139190 Book/Audio $10.99

Also available:

AMERICAN TUNES
arr. Eric Baumgartner
MID-ELEMENTARY LEVEL
00406755 Book only $6.99

BLUES AND BOOGIE
Carolyn Miller
MID-ELEMENTARY LEVEL
00406764 Book only $5.99

CHRISTMAS CAROLS
arr. Carolyn Miller
MID-ELEMENTARY LEVEL
00406763 Book only $6.99

CHRISTMAS CLASSICS
arr. Eric Baumgartner
MID-ELEMENTARY LEVEL
00416827 Book only $6.99
00416826 Book/Audio $12.99

CHRISTMAS FAVORITES
arr. Eric Baumgartner
MID-ELEMENTARY LEVEL
00416723 Book only $7.99
00416724 Book/Audio $12.99

FAMILIAR TUNES
arr. Glenda Austin
MID-ELEMENTARY LEVEL
00406761 Book only $6.99

HYMNS
arr. Glenda Austin
MID-ELEMENTARY LEVEL
00406762 Book only $6.99

JEWISH FAVORITES
arr. Eric Baumgartner
MID-ELEMENTARY LEVEL
00416755 Book only $5.99

RECITAL PIECES
Carolyn Miller
MID-ELEMENTARY LEVEL
00416540 Book only $5.99

SONGS FROM MANY LANDS
arr. Carolyn C. Setliff
MID-ELEMENTARY LEVEL
00416688 Book only $5.99

WILLIS MUSIC

EXCLUSIVELY DISTRIBUTED BY

HAL•LEONARD®

Complete song lists online at
www.halleonard.com

0218